PIANO·VOCAL·GUITAR

2nd Edition

THE DEFINITIVE
Rock 'n' Roll
COLLECTION (1955-1968)

95 Vintage Classics

GW00570268

ISBN 0-88188-833-8

HAL•LEONARD®
CORPORATION
7777 W. BLUEMOUND RD. P.O. BOX 13819 MILWAUKEE, WI 53213

Visit Hal Leonard Online at
www.halleonard.com

THE DEFINITIVE

Rock 'n' Roll
COLLECTION

ALL DAY AND ALL OF THE NIGHT

Words and Music by
RAY DAVIES

1. I'm not con-tent to be with you __ in the
2. I be-lieve to that you and me __ last for-
3. I be-lieve to that you and me __ last for-

day-time __
ev-er __
ev-er __

Girl I want to
Oh yeh all day and
Oh yeh all day and

be with you __ all of the time __
night-time yours, __ leave me nev-er __
night-time yours, __ leave me nev-er __

ALL SHOOK UP

Words and Music by OTIS BLACKWELL
and ELVIS PRESLEY

AT THE HOP

Words and Music by ARTHUR SINGER,
JOHN MADARA and DAVID WHITE

BIG GIRLS DON'T CRY

Words and Music by BOB CREWE
and BOB GAUDIO

BARBARA ANN

Words and Music by
FRED FASSERT

Bright Rock

(Ba, ba, ba, ba, ___ Ba' - 'bra Ann. Ba, ba, ba, ba, ___ Ba' - 'bra Ann)
Ba' - 'bra

Ann, _____ take ___ my ___ hand. _____ Ba' - 'bra

Ann, _____ you got me rock-in' and a - roll-in', rock-

BE-BOP-A-LULA

Words and Music by TEX DAVIS
and GENE VINCENT

Moderately slow Rock

BE TRUE TO YOUR SCHOOL

Words and Music by BRIAN WILSON
and MIKE LOVE

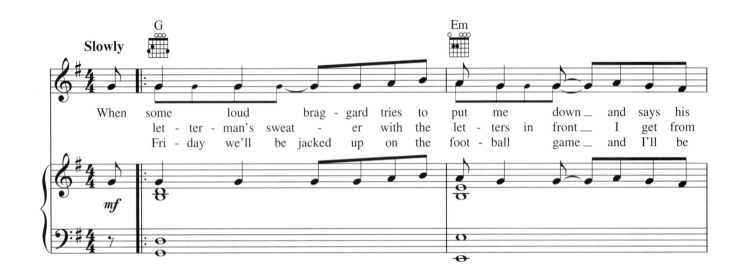

When some loud brag-gard tries to put me down __ and says his
let - ter - man's sweat - er with the let - ters in front __ I get from
Fri - day we'll be jacked up on the foot - ball game __ and I'll be

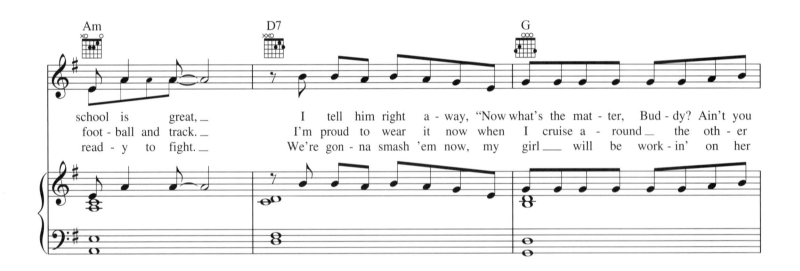

school is great, __ I tell him right a - way, "Now what's the mat - ter, Bud - dy? Ain't you
foot - ball and track. __ I'm proud to wear it now when I cruise a - round __ the oth - er
read - y to fight. We're gon - na smash 'em now, my girl __ will be work - in' on her

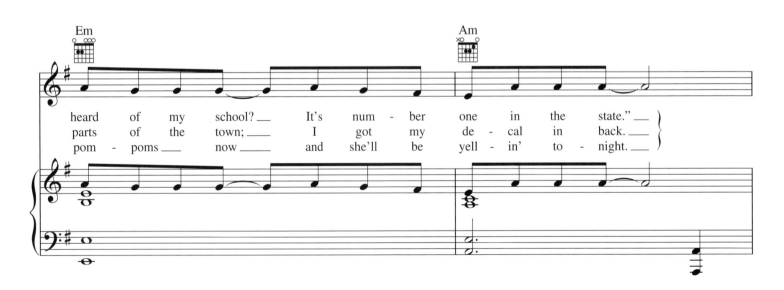

heard of my school? __ It's num - ber one in the state." __
parts of the town; __ I got my de - cal in back. __
pom - poms __ now __ and she'll be yell - in' to - night. __

BLUE SUEDE SHOES

Words and Music by
CARL LEE PERKINS

Well, it's one for the mon-ey, two for the show,

three to get read-y, now go, cat, go! But don't you

BLUEBERRY HILL

Words and Music by AL LEWIS,
LARRY STOCK and VINCENT ROSE

BOBBY'S GIRL

Words and Music by GARY KLEIN
and HENRY HOFFMAN

BREAD AND BUTTER

Words and Music by LARRY PARKS
and JAY TURNBOW

1. I like bread and
2.-4. *(See additional lyrics)*

but - ter, I like toast and jam.

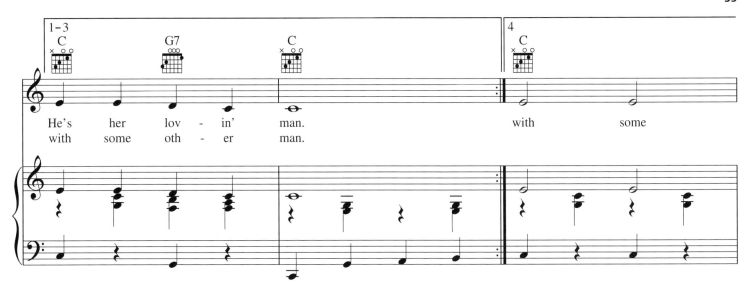

He's her lov - in' man.   with some
with some oth - er man.

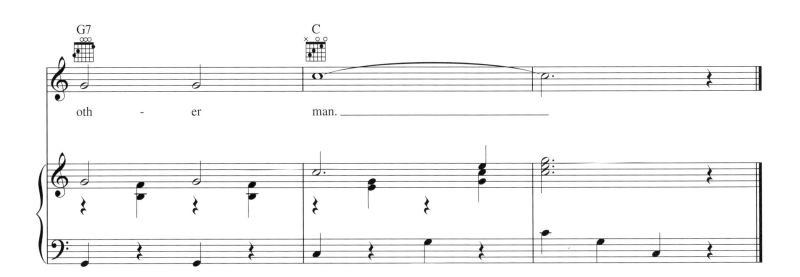

oth - er man. _____

Additional Lyrics

2. She don't cook mashed potatoes,
   Don't cook T-bone steak.
   Don't feed me peanut butter.
   She knows that I can't take.

3. Got home early one mornin'.
   Much to my surprise
   She was eatin' chicken and dumplins
   With some other guy.

4. No more bread and butter,
   No more toast and jam.
   I found my baby eatin'
   With some other man.

BOOK OF LOVE

Words and Music by WARREN DAVIS,
GEORGE MALONE and CHARLES PATRICK

Tell me, tell me, tell me, oh, who wrote the book of love? I've
got to know the an-swer. Was it some-one from a-bove? I won-der, won-der
who, _____ who, who wrote the book of love? _____

BYE BYE LOVE

Words and Music by FELICE BRYANT
and BOUDLEAUX BRYANT

Moderately fast

CATCH A WAVE

Words and Music by BRIAN WILSON
and MIKE LOVE

CHANTILLY LACE

Moderate Boogie Woogie

Words and Music by
J.P. RICHARDSON

Ain't noth-in' in this world like a big eyed girl ___ to make me

act so fun-ny, make me spend my mon-ey, make me feel real loose like a

long-necked goose, like a girl. *Spoken:* Oh, Baby, *that's-a what I like.*

girl. *Spoken:* Oh, Baby, *that's-a what I like.*

COME GO WITH ME

Words and Music by
C.E. QUICK

Love, love me, dar-lin', come and go__ with me,__ Please don't send me

'way be-yond__ the sea;__ I need you, dar-lin', So come go__ with

DO WAH DIDDY DIDDY

Words and Music by JEFF BARRY
and ELLIE GREENWICH

DO YOU WANT TO DANCE?

Words and Music by
BOBBY FREEMAN

DON'T BE CRUEL
(To a Heart That's True)

Words and Music by OTIS BLACKWELL
and ELVIS PRESLEY

Moderately, with half-time feel

You know I can be found
Ba-by, if I made you mad
Don't stop think-in' of
Instrumental solo

me.
sit-tin' home all a-lone.
for some-thing I might have said,
Don't make me feel this way.

If
Come

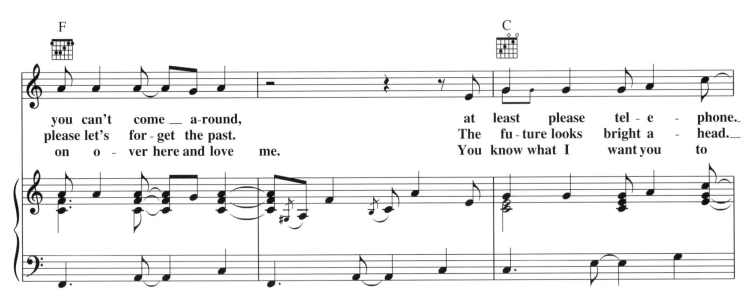

you can't come a-round,
please let's for-get the past.
on o-ver here and love me.

at least please tel-e-phone.
The fu-ture looks bright a-head.
You know what I want you to

DREAM BABY
(How Long Must I Dream)

Words and Music by
CINDY WALKER

DREAM LOVER

Words and Music by
BOBBY DARIN

EARTH ANGEL

Words and Music by
JESSE BELVIN

DUKE OF EARL

Words and Music by EARL EDWARDS,
EUGENE DIXON and BERNICE WILLIAMS

As ___ I _____ walk through this world,
When _____ I hold ___ you,

noth-ing can stop the Duke of Earl. ___ And you _____ are my
you ___ will be the Duch-ess of Earl. When I walk _____ through my

girl, _____ and no one can hurt you. Yes,
Duke-dom, the par - a - dise we will share.

EIGHT DAYS A WEEK

Words and Music by JOHN LENNON
and PAUL McCARTNEY

Ooh I need your love, babe,
guess you know it's true,___
Hope you need my love, babe,
just like I need you.___

Love you ev-'ry day, girl,___
al - ways on my mind.___
One thing I can say, girl,___
love you all the time.___

EVERYDAY

Words and Music by NORMAN PETTY
and CHARLES HARDIN

Ev - 'ry day   it's a - get - tin' clos - er,
Ev - 'ry day   it's a - get - tin' fast - er,

go - ing fast - er than a roll - er coast - er.
ev - 'ry - one said "Go on up and ask her." } Love like

yours will tru - ly come my way. _____

FEVER

Words and Music by JOHN DAVENPORT
and EDDIE COOLEY

Verse 3 Romeo loved Juliet
Juliet she felt the same,
When he put his arms around her, he said,
"Julie, baby you're my flame."

Chorus Thou givest fever, when we kisseth
Fever with my flaming youth,
Fever – I'm afire
Fever, yea I burn forsooth.

Verse 4 Captain Smith and Pocahantas
Had a very mad affair,
When her Daddy tried to kill him, she said,
"Daddy-o don't you dare."

Chorus Give me fever, with his kisses,
Fever when he holds me tight.
Fever – I'm his Missus
Oh Daddy won't you treat him right.

Verse 5 Now you've listened to my story
Here's the point that I have made:
Chicks were born to give you fever
Be it fahrenheit or centigrade.

Chorus They give you fever when you kiss them,
Fever if you live and learn.
Fever – till you sizzle
What a lovely way to burn.

GET A JOB

Words and Music by EARL BEAL, RICHARD LEWIS,
RAYMOND EDWARDS and WILLIAM HORTON

GLORIA

Words and Music by
VAN MORRISON

GOOD LOVIN'

Words and Music by RUDY CLARK
and ARTHUR RESNICK

Well,__ I was feel -

- in'
- by

(Instrumental)- - - - - - - - - - -

oh _____ so _____ bad _____ now.
woah _____ squeeze me tight.

So I asked my fam' - ly doc - tor 'bout what I _____ had _____
Said don't-cha' don't you want your dad - dy to be all _____

GOD ONLY KNOWS

Words and Music by BRIAN WILSON
and TONY ASHER

GREAT BALLS OF FIRE

Words and Music by OTIS BLACKWELL
and JACK HAMMER

THE GREAT PRETENDER

Words and Music by
BUCK RAM

Oh, yes___ I'm the great pre-tend-er, ___ Pre-tend-in' I'm___ do-in' well; My need is such,___ I pre-tend too much, I'm lone-ly but no-one can tell. Oh,

HEARTBREAK HOTEL

Words and Music by MAE BOREN AXTON,
TOMMY DURDEN and ELVIS PRESLEY

HOUND DOG

Words and Music by JERRY LEIBER
and MIKE STOLLER

Moderate Shuffle

You ain't noth-in' but a Hound Dog,__ cry-in' all the time.

You ain't noth-in' but a Hound Dog,__ cry-in' all the time.

Well__ you ain't

To Coda

I GET AROUND

Words and Music by BRIAN WILSON
and MIKE LOVE

I GOT YOU
(I Feel Good)

Words and Music by
JAMES BROWN

('Til)
I KISSED YOU

Words and Music by
DON EVERLY

Nev - er felt like this __ un - til I kissed you.
Things have real - ly changed __ since I kissed you.

How did I ex - ist __ un - til I kissed you?
My life's not the same __ now that I kissed you.

IN MY ROOM

Words and Music by BRIAN WILSON
and GARY USHER

I WANT YOU, I NEED YOU, I LOVE YOU

Words by MAURICE MYSELS
Music by IRA KOSLOFF

Moderately Slow

Hold me close, __ hold me tight; __ make me thrill __ with de -light. __ Let me know __ where I stand __ from the

start. __ I Want You, I Need You, I Love You __ with all my

heart. Ev - 'ry time __ that you're near __ all my cares __ dis- ap -pear. __ Dar-ling,

IN THE STILL OF THE NITE
(I'll Remember)

Words and Music by
FRED PARRIS

love, _____ love __ you so, _____ prom-ise I'll

nev - er _____ let __ you go, _____ in the still _____ of the

nite. _____ I re -

mem - ber _____ that nite in May, _____ the

IT'S MY PARTY

Words and Music by HERB WIENER,
WALLY GOLD and JOHN GLUCK, JR.

Moderately bright

No - bod - y knows___ where - my John - ny has gone,___ "But
Play all my rec - ords, keep danc - ing all night,___ But
Ju - dy and John - ny just walked thru the door,___

Ju - dy left___ the same time.
leave me a - lone___ for a - while,
Like a queen___ with her king,

Why was he
'Til John - ny's
Oh, John what a

hold - ing her hand,___ when he's sup - posed___ to be mine?___
danc - ing with me,___ I've got no, rea - son to smile.___
birth - day sur - prise,___ Ju - dy's wear - ing his ring.___

It's my par - ty, and I'll cry if I want___ to, Cry if I want___ to,

Cry if I want___ to, You would cry, too, if it hap - pened to

you.

IT'S ONLY MAKE BELIEVE

Words and Music by CONWAY TWITTY
and JACK NANCE

JUST ONE LOOK

Words and Music by DORIS PAYNE
and GREGORY CARROLL

KANSAS CITY

Words and Music by JERRY LEIBER
and MIKE STOLLER

LIMBO ROCK

Words and Music by BILLY STRANGE
and JON SHELDON

lim - bo boy __ and girl all a - round the lim - bo world gon - na
spread your lim - bo feet, then you move to lim - bo beat. Lim - bo
self a lim - bo girl, give that chick a lim - bo whirl. There's a

Ev - 'ry

LAND OF A THOUSAND DANCES

Words and Music by
CHRIS KENNER

LITTLE DARLIN'

Words and Music by
MAURICE WILLIAMS

(May be spoken over repeat:)

My dear, I need your love to call my own
And never do wrong; and to hold in mine your little hand.
I'll know too soon that I'll love again.
Please come back to me.

LOLLIPOP

Words and Music by BEVERLY ROSS
and JULIUS DIXON

THE LOCO-MOTION

Words and Music by GERRY GOFFIN
and CAROLE KING

LONG TALL SALLY

Words and Music by ENOTRIS JOHNSON,
RICHARD PENNIMAN and ROBERT BLACKWELL

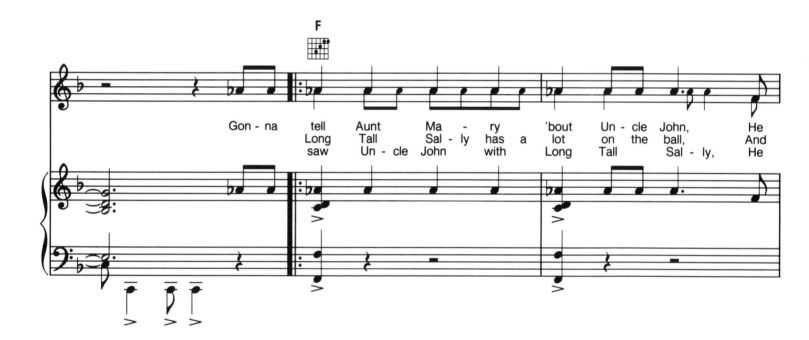

Gon - na tell Aunt Ma - ry 'bout Un - cle John, He
Long Tall Sal - ly has a lot on the ball, And
saw Un - cle John has with Long Tall Sal - ly, He

says he has the blues, But he has a lot of fun, Oh,
no - bod - y cares if she's long and tall, Oh,
saw Aunt Ma - ry com - in' And he ducked back in the al - ley, Oh,

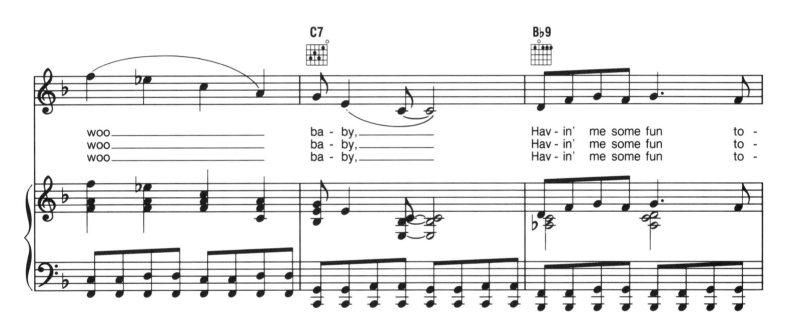

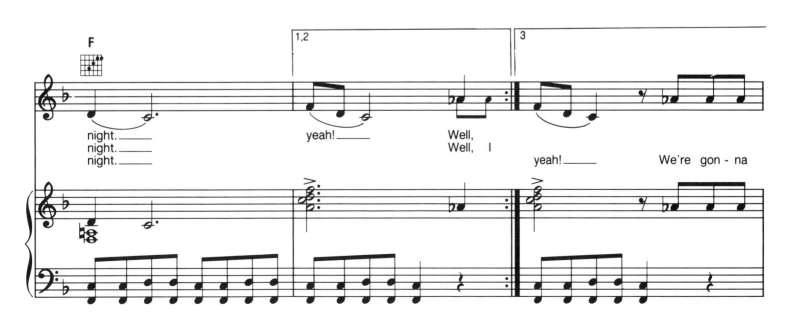

NORMAN

Words and Music by
JOHN D. LOUDERMILK

LOUIE, LOUIE

Words and Music by
RICHARD BERRY

LOVE ME TENDER

Words and Music by ELVIS PRESLEY
and VERA MATSON

LOVING YOU

Words and Music by JERRY LEIBER
and MIKE STOLLER

*Even eighth notes.

MY BOYFRIEND'S BACK

Words and Music by ROBERT FELDMAN,
GERALD GOLDSTEIN and RICHARD GOTTEHRER

My boy-friend's back, and you're gon-na be in trou-ble.
He's been gone for ___ such a long ___ time. ___

(Hey, la, hey la, my boy-friend's back.)

When you see him com-in', bet-ter
Now he's back ___ and ___

(Hey la, hey la, my boy-friend's back.)

cut on the dou-ble.
things will be fine. ___

You're

MY PRAYER

Music by GEORGES BOULANGER
Lyric and Musical Adaptation by JIMMY KENNEDY

ONLY THE LONELY
(Know the Way I Feel)

Words and Music by ROY ORBISON
and JOE MELSON

PEGGY SUE

Words and Music by JERRY ALLISON,
NORMAN PETTY and BUDDY HOLLY

Peg - gy Sue;_____ Oh, well, I

love you gal,_____ and I need you, Peg - gy Sue._____

I love you,_____

Peg - gy Sue,_____ With a love so rare and true,_____ Oh, well, I

Oh, Peg - gy, _____ My Peg - gy Sue; _____

Oh, well, I love you, gal, _____

Yes, I want you, Peg - gy Sue. _____

ROCK AROUND THE CLOCK

Words and Music by MAX C. FREEDMAN
and JIMMY DeKNIGHT

A ROSE AND A BABY RUTH

Words and Music by
JOHN D. LOUDERMILK

Moderately slow

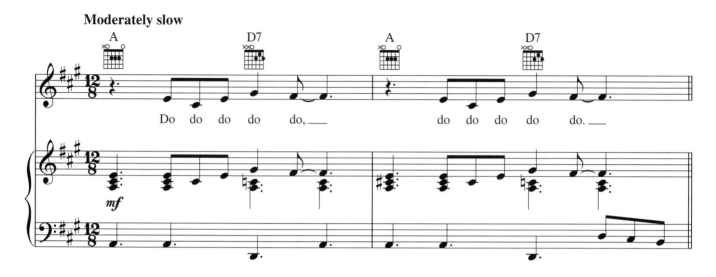

Do do do do do, ___ do do do do do. ___

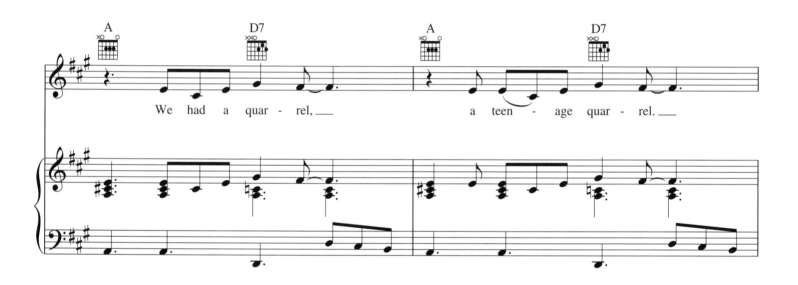

We had a quar-rel, ___ a teen-age quar-rel. ___

Now I'm as blue ___ as I know how ___ to be.

RUBY BABY

Words and Music by JERRY LEIBER
and MIKE STOLLER

RUNAWAY

Words and Music by DEL SHANNON
and MAX CROOK

Moderately Bright

As I walk a long___ I won-der what went wrong with our love, a love that was ___ so strong.

And as I still walk on ___ I think of the things we've done ___ to-

SEA OF LOVE

Words and Music by GEORGE KHOURY
and PHILIP BAPTISTE

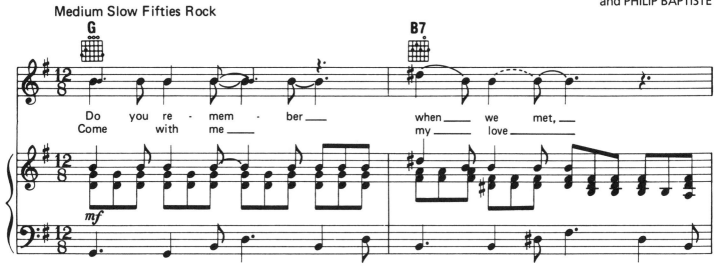

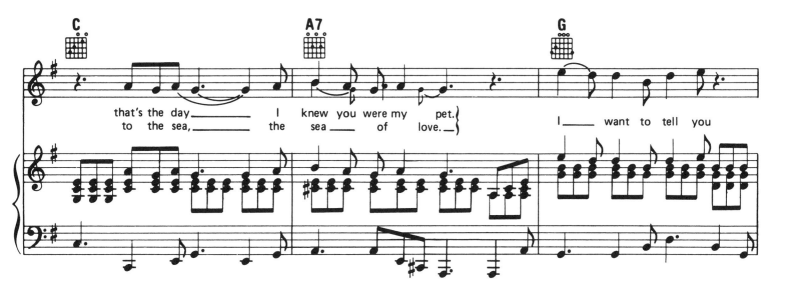

Come _____ with me_____

to _____ the sea _____ of love._____

D.C. al Coda (verse 1)

CODA

Guitar Tacet

Come _____ with me _____

to _____ the sea _____ of

SAVE THE LAST DANCE FOR ME

Words and Music by DOC POMUS
and MORT SHUMAN

SEARCHIN'

Words and Music by JERRY LEIBER
and MIKE STOLLER

SEE YOU LATER, ALLIGATOR

Words and Music by
ROBERT GUIDRY

THE SHOOP SHOOP SONG
(It's in His Kiss)

Words and Music by
RUDY CLARK

(Seven Little Girls)
SITTING IN THE BACK SEAT

Words by BOB HILLIARD
Music by LEE POCKRISS

SHOUT

Words and Music by O'KELLY ISLEY,
RONALD ISLEY and RUDOLPH ISLEY

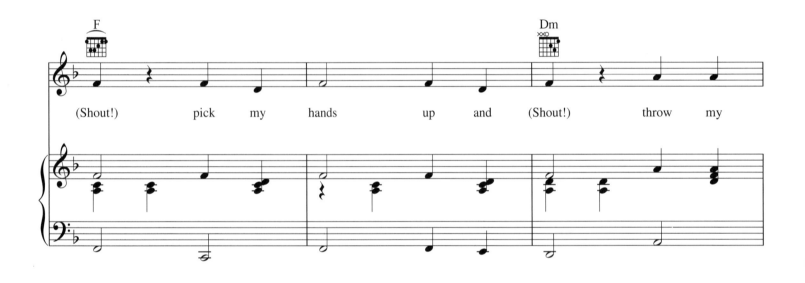

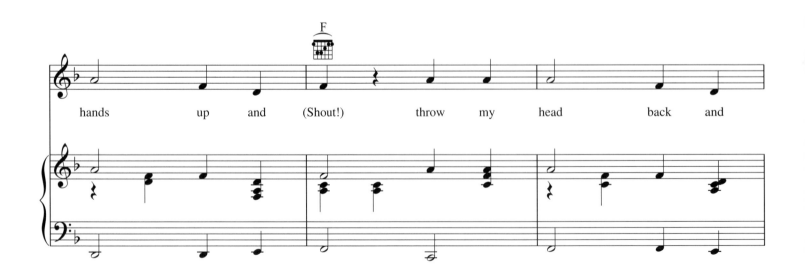

SINCE I DON'T HAVE YOU

Words and Music by JAMES BEAUMONT,
JANET VOGEL, JOSEPH VERSCHAREN,
WALTER LESTER, LENNIE MARTIN,
JOSEPH ROCK and JOHN TAYLOR

SINCERELY

Words and Music by ALAN FREED
and HARVEY FUQUA

SINGING THE BLUES

Words and Music by
MELVIN ENDSLEY

cry _____ o - ver you ___ well, I nev - er felt more like

run - ning a - way ___ but why should I go ___ 'cause I could - n't stay ___ with -

out you. You got me sing - ing the blues. _____

___ Well, I blues. _____

SPLISH SPLASH

Words and Music by BOBBY DARIN
and MURRAY KAUFMAN

STAND BY ME

Words and Music by BEN E. KING,
JERRY LEIBER and MIKE STOLLER

SUMMER IN THE CITY

Words and Music by JOHN SEBASTIAN,
STEVE BOONE and MARK SEBASTIAN

STAY

Words and Music by
MAURICE WILLIAMS

Moderately

Dance _____ just a lit-tle bit long-er. _____

Please, please, please, please tell___ me that you're go-in' to. _____ Now your

dad-dy don't mind, _____ and your mom-my don't mind. _____

SUNSHINE OF YOUR LOVE

Words and Music by JACK BRUCE,
PETE BROWN and ERIC CLAPTON

SURFER GIRL

Words and Music by
BRIAN WILSON

SURFIN' U.S.A.

Words by BRIAN WILSON
Music by CHUCK BERRY

TEARS ON MY PILLOW

Words and Music by SYLVESTER BRADFORD
and AL LEWIS

A TEENAGER IN LOVE

Words and Music by DOC POMUS
and MORT SHUMAN

TEEN ANGEL

Words and Music by
JEAN SURREY

THAT'LL BE THE DAY

Words and Music by JERRY ALLISON,
NORMAN PETTY and BUDDY HOLLY

Well, you give me all your lov-in' and your tur-tle-dov-in', All___ your hugs an' kiss-es an' your mon-ey too;___ Well, you know you love me, ba-by, Un-til you tell me, may-be, that some day, well, I'll be through! Well,___ That-'ll Be The Day, when you say, good-bye, Yes,___ That-'ll Be The Day, when

TRAVELIN' MAN

Words and Music by
JERRY FULLER

UNDER THE BOARDWALK

Words and Music by ARTIE RESNICK
and KENNY YOUNG

THE TWIST

Words and Music by
HANK BALLARD

TWIST AND SHOUT

Words and Music by BERT RUSSELL
and PHIL MEDLEY

VENUS

Words and Music by
EDWARD MARSHALL

WAKE UP LITTLE SUSIE

Words and Music by BOUDLEAUX BRYANT
and FELICE BRYANT

Rock Tempo

WHY DO FOOLS FALL IN LOVE

Words and Music by MORRIS LEVY
and FRANKIE LYMON

WILD THING

Words and Music by
CHIP TAYLOR

WILLIE AND THE HAND JIVE

Words and Music by
JOHNNY OTIS

1. I know a cat named Way - Out Wil - lie. He got a
2. Pa - pa told Wil - lie, "You'll ru - in my home. He's
3. Ma - ma, ma - ma, look at Un - cle Joe. Now
4. Doc - tor and a law - yer and an In - dian chief. They had a
(5.) Wil - lie and Mil - lie got mar - ried last fall.

YA YA

Words and Music by MORRIS LEVY
and CLARENCE LEWIS

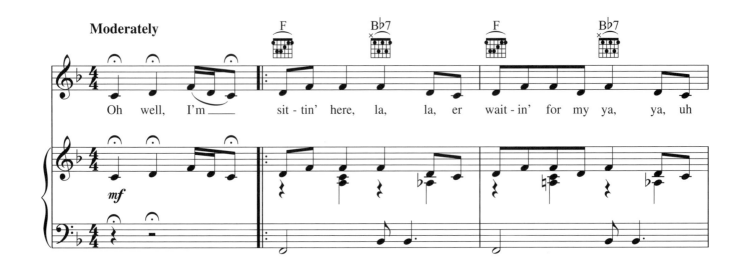

Oh well, I'm ___ sit-tin' here, la, la, er wait-in' for my ya, ya, uh

huh, uh huh. Er sit-tin' here, la, la, er wait-in' for my ya, ya, uh

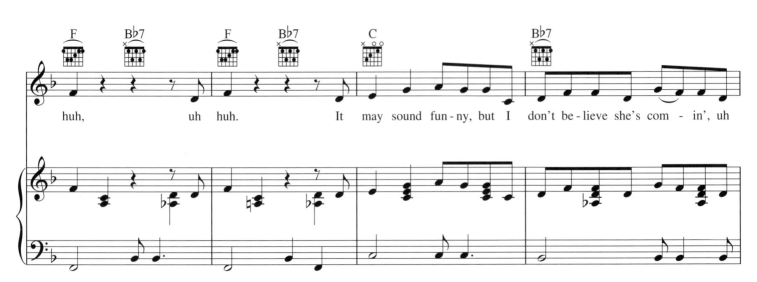

huh, uh huh. It may sound fun-ny, but I don't be-lieve she's com - in', uh

YOUNG LOVE

Words and Music by
RIC CARTEY

WOOLY BULLY

Words and Music by
DOMINGO SAMUDIO

Bul - ly

Additional Lyrics

2. Hatty told Matty
   Let's don't take no chance,
   Let's not be L 7
   Come and learn to dance
   Wooly bully — wooly bully —
   Wooly bully — wooly bully — wooly bully.

3 Matty told Hatty
   That's the thing to do,
   Get yo' someone really
   To pull the wool with you —
   Wooly bully — wooly bully
   Wooly bully — wooly bully — wooly bully.